WHAT IF YOU WERE ON THE EUROPEAN FRONT IN WORLD WAR II?

AN INTERACTIVE HISTORY ADVENTURE

by Matt Doeden

CAPSTONE PRESS
a capstone imprint

Published by You Choose, an imprint of Capstone
1710 Roe Crest Drive, North Mankato, Minnesota 56003
capstonepub.com

Library of Congress Cataloging-in-Publication Data
Names: Doeden, Matt, author.
Title: What if you were on the European front in World War II? : an interactive
history adventure / by Matt Doeden. Other titles: What if you were on the
European front in World War 2?
Description: North Mankato, Minesota : You Choose, an imprint of Capstone,
[2023] | Series: You choose: World War II frontlines | Includes bibliographical
references. | Audience: Ages 8-12 | Audience: Grades 4-6 | Summary: "Adolf
Hitler's Nazi forces have violently conquered lands across Europe. They have
created brutal camps where Jews, prisoners of war, and other perceived enemies
work themselves to death. You are fighting against the Nazis on the frontlines in
Europe. YOU CHOOSE what part will you play in fighting for freedom. Are you
willing to pay the ultimate price?"— Provided by publisher.
Identifiers: LCCN 2022041599 (print) | LCCN 2022041600 (ebook) | ISBN
9781666390933 (hardcover) | ISBN 9781666390926 (paperback) | ISBN
9781666391084 (pdf)
Subjects: LCSH: World War, 1939-1945—Campaigns—Europe—Juvenile
literature. | Plot-your-own stories.
Classification: LCC D743 .D55 2023 (print) | LCC D743 (ebook) | DDC
940.54/21—dc23/eng/20220830
LC record available at https://lccn.loc.gov/2022041599
LC ebook record available at https://lccn.loc.gov/2022041600

Editorial Credits
Editor: Mandy Robbins; Designer: Hilary Wacholz; Media Researcher: Jo Miller;
Production Specialist: Tori Abraham

Image Credits
Alamy: Matteo Omied, 11; Associated Press, 47; Shutterstock: Andreas Gradin,
38, Andrei Metelev, 84, Everett Collection, 4, 21, 67, 102, Grisha Bruev, 40, l.glz.
ttlphotos, 55, Mata Norway, 30, Mike Pellinni, 14, Milan Sommer, 105, Pierre Jean
Durieu, 72, Red_Baron, 106, Vastram, 22, Vilenia, 29; Wikimedia: 44th Bomb
Group Photograph Collection, 58, Signal Corps Archive, 99, U.S. Army, 76, 82,
United Kingdom Government, 9, U.S. Office of War Information Overseas Picture
Division, 70, U.S. Air Force, Cover, 53, U.S. Army Signal Corps, Cover, 90, U.S.
Navy, Cover, 1

Design Elements
Shutterstock: Roman Amanov

TABLE OF CONTENTS

Soldiers at the Battle of the Bulge

ABOUT YOUR ADVENTURE

YOU are on the front lines of World War II (1939–1945). In Europe, the Allied forces are fighting to stop Nazi Germany and the other Axis powers from conquering the continent. War planes fill the skies. Tanks roll over dirt and mud. Battles rage across the landscape. YOU CHOOSE which paths to take. Your choices will guide the story. Live or die. Succeed or fail. Do you have what it takes to do your part for the Allies?

• Turn the page to begin your adventure.

CHAPTER 1
WAR IN EUROPE

The chatter of machine guns. The booming explosions of bombs. The roar of aircraft engines. War rages all around you. The Allied forces, including the United States, Great Britain, France, and Russia, battle the Axis nations of Germany, Japan, and Italy. You're in Europe, where some of the most intense fighting is tearing the continent apart.

The Axis powers are sweeping through Europe to occupy as much land as they can. You and the rest of the people fighting for the Allied forces are determined to stop them.

You have your orders. You check your gear, review your maps, and prepare yourself for the mission ahead of you. It's time to fight. Your task won't be easy. There's a good chance that you won't make it back alive. But you'll have people by your side, and you'll work together to perform your mission and do your part to tilt the war in favor of the Allies.

Are you ready to enter the biggest war the world has ever seen? Every battle hangs in the balance. Where will you fight?

- To join a secret mission to destroy an important German factory, turn to page 8.

- To take control of a B-24 Liberator on a bombing mission, turn to page 44.

- To join in the rescue of the trapped U.S. "Lost Battalion," turn to page 73.

CHAPTER 2

OPERATION GUNNERSIDE

A blast of icy air slaps your face as you perform one final check of your gear. The bay doors of the Halifax bomber plane open, revealing a moonlit, snow-covered Norwegian landscape below.

"This is it, men," you shout over the roar of the wind. Your squad of six men makes its final preparations. "It's time. The Germans control the land below. We have to be on constant guard. We cannot let them spot us. Let's go!"

A Halifax bomber

You lead the way, launching yourself out of the open bay doors. Your squad is right behind you. Together, you plummet through the bitterly cold air toward the ground below.

You wait as long as you can before opening your parachute. You can't risk being spotted by enemy patrols in the area.

Turn the page.

Finally, as the ground rushes toward you, you open the chute. Your body jerks as the chute opens and the lines tighten. Just a few moments later, your boots touch down with a crunch on the snowy, rugged ground. One by one, your squad mates land beside you. Like you, all of them are Norwegian. They're ready to do whatever it takes to fight the German invaders. Your mission is called Operation Gunnerside.

Once everyone is safe on the ground, you say, "Okay, men, the Germans have captured a plant that can produce a substance called heavy water. It's critical to their efforts to build atomic weapons. Our mission is simple. We destroy the plant with explosives. If we succeed, it could set back their research efforts by months or even years."

Knut, one of your men, unfolds a map on the ground. "Here is the plant," he says, jabbing his finger to a point on the map. "It's well defended. It sits on an open cliff ledge. There's a sheer drop below it and a sheer rise above."

"We have two choices," you explain. "We can travel to the top of the ridge and drop down, or we can attack from below, climbing the cliff face."

Vemork hydroelectric power plant in Tinn, Norway

Turn the page.

"It will be easier to stay hidden if we come in from below," says Leif.

"But coming in from higher ground puts us in a stronger position," says Fredrik.

Either way, you'll travel over the snowy landscape on cross-country skis. As you strap your feet into your skis, you consider your options. Neither choice will be easy. British forces tried a similar mission not long ago. They didn't make it.

Your team is ready to go. They just need orders from you.

- To attack from below the plant, go to page 13.

- To head for the top of the ridge and attack from above, turn to page 15.

"Leif is right," you decide. "We'll attack from below. We can use the cover of night to climb the cliff. From there, we can set explosives to disable the plant."

After meeting up with several men who were already on the ground, you are ready. As the wind howls and the snow swirls around you, your 11-man team heads out into the snowy night. It's slow progress. After an hour, you can barely feel your toes. But you press on, knowing that darkness will be key to your success.

The path takes you to a small, swiftly moving river. "The water isn't high here," Knut says. "We can cross easily."

The crossing doesn't look dangerous. But the water will be ice cold. Being cold and wet could be dangerous for you and your men.

Turn the page.

You glance up and down the river, searching for a better option. Perhaps you could work your way along the banks in hopes of finding a better way across. It could keep you dry but will cost you time.

- To cross the river here, turn to page 18.
- To look for another way, turn to page 30.

"Let's come in from above. We'll be able to get a good view of the plant's guards and defenses from above. We can plan our attack better if we know exactly what we're getting into."

The first job is to meet up with a small team of men already on the ground. They've laid a lot of the groundwork for you. They've got your supplies—including the explosive charges—and they know the land.

Eleven men strong, you head out into the winter night on cross-country skis. All of you are Norwegian, and the harsh, snowy terrain is your home. You track along a high ridge, following the land as it rises through dense forest.

Turn the page.

"There it is," says Knut after several hours of hard travel. Your team pulls up to the top of a high ridge, staying hidden in the shadows of the trees. Moonlight falls on the heavy water plant below. It's tucked in on the shelf of a ridge, protected by cliffs from above and below.

"There's the rail line they use to transport the heavy water," Leif points out. A bridge crosses a gap in the ravine. It's the easiest way in and the most heavily guarded. "We'll want to stay clear of that."

Knut is unpacking climbing gear. It's a long drop down from here. Even in daylight, it would be a challenging descent. But you know your men are up to the task.

"We've only got an hour or two before sunrise," Knut says. "We should get moving."

Fredrik's gaze is fixed on the shelf below you. "We don't know their patrols. Or their strength. It might be worth waiting to see if we can learn anything."

Should you keep watching awhile longer? Or are you ready to move on?

- To continue observing the plant, turn to page 26.
- To begin your descent, turn to page 37.

You don't have time to look around. In a few hours, the sun will rise. You need to stage your attack before that happens. "Everyone across," you order. "Move quickly."

You lead your team across the shallow river. It's an easy crossing. The water level is low, and you're all safely across in a minute. Even though your feet are cold and wet after the crossing, it won't slow you down. From the river, you follow the railroad tracks that lead toward the plant You don't encounter a single guard along the way. Everything is going according to plan.

You finally arrive at the plant with plenty of time before sunrise. Its placement along the ravine makes it look like a fortress. There's no easy way to approach.

"Straight ahead, there's a small bridge that crosses the ravine," Leif points out. "That would be our easiest approach."

"The bridge is sure to be guarded," says Knut. He points to the rocky cliff below the plant. "That's our way in."

The cliff is a sheer rock face, slick with snow and ice. You're not sure if climbing that in the dark of night is any safer than openly crossing the bridge. But it's probably unguarded. The Germans wouldn't expect anyone to try to approach from that direction.

- To cross the bridge, turn to page 20.
- To try climbing the cliff, turn to page 22.

You don't like the looks of that cliff at all. You nod toward the bridge. "We go that way. We move quickly. Even if the bridge is guarded, it might just be one or two men. They won't be expecting us, so if we storm it, we can set our explosives and get out before the Germans have the chance to react."

You can see uncertainty in the body language of your men, but no one questions your orders. You approach the bridge, preparing for your charge. Your heart is racing. You only get one shot at this. It's time. You give your team a nod and signal them to move.

In silence, you and your men charge across. For a moment, you think that maybe nobody has spotted you.

Then you hear the rattle of gunfire. The bridge is guarded better than you'd thought.

You have no cover and nowhere to retreat. Your mission is a failure, and your whole team pays for it with their lives.

THE END

To follow another path, turn to page 7.

To learn more about the European front, turn to page 100.

Your crew is highly trained. The cliff will be a challenge. But it's nothing your men can't handle. "Let's climb," you order.

In the dark, still night, every sound stands out. You hear the hum of machinery above.

Your heartbeat quickens at the scraping of gloves and boots as you ascend the cliff. Each of you carries a pack with explosives on your back, making the climb that much harder. Leif is your best climber. He goes ahead of the rest of the team, setting a few anchors and ropes as he climbs. You'll need them for the trip back down—if you make it that far.

Finally, you reach the top. As you near the cliff's edge, you hear the crunch of boots walking on snow above you. Maybe you should wait a few minutes before finishing the climb. But you're not sure how much longer you and your men can hang on here.

- To wait a few minutes, turn to page 24.
- To quietly pull yourself up, turn to page 28.

You signal to your men to hold still. Your arms ache, and you can't feel your fingers. But you need to let the patrol pass. A minute passes . . . then two. The sound of footsteps has disappeared. You're alone.

"Let's go," you whisper. Your team moves swiftly, hauling themselves up over the ledge onto solid ground.

Your orders are to attach explosives to the plant's electrolysis chambers. These large tanks hold most of the plant's heavy water, preparing it for use as atomic fuel. "There's a lot of open ground between us and those chambers," Knut observes. "But look. Their loading facility is right there. That's where they load the heavy water onto railcars. Destroying that would be much easier."

It would be safer to destroy the loading station. But would it be enough to slow down the German research? Is it worth the risk to blow up the chambers instead?

- To blow up the loading station, turn to page 33.
- To move in toward the chambers, turn to page 35.

"Hold up," you order. "Let's watch. Maybe we can get a better sense of their patrols before we descend."

You spend the next 20 minutes carefully observing the plant. It's hard to get a complete picture in the darkness. But you manage to pick out a few watch stations and get a sense of the patrols. Leif finds a route down that's well concealed from the German watch stations.

Armed with this knowledge, you begin your descent. With Leif leading the group, you make your way quickly and carefully down the rock face. Nobody spots you, and your boots touch down on the snow with a satisfying crunch.

"There," you whisper, pointing at the plant's electrolysis chambers. "That's our target. Set the charges."

The team snaps into action, placing the explosives on the large tanks that are critical to the heavy water production. With the long fuses lit, you hurry back to the cliff to climb up. You should be long gone by the time the explosives go off. Leif leads the way. One by one, others follow. You'll be the last one up the cliff.

That's when you're spotted. You hear shouting, followed by a loud alarm.

"GO!" you yell. But you know your men are already moving as quickly as they can. You have only minutes before the Germans arrive. Can you all make it up in time?

- To head up the cliff, turn to page 40.

- To create a diversion to give your men more time, turn to page 42.

You're not sure your arms can hold on any longer. "Quietly," you whisper.

As silently as you can, you haul your body up over the cliff, onto solid ground. Your men follow. But as one man pulls himself up, he accidentally knocks loose a large piece of rock. It tumbles loudly down the cliff face, crashing and smashing into the cliff as it falls.

Your heart sinks as a light suddenly appears near your position. You hear muddled shouting in German and footsteps approach.

"Stop! Don't move!" shouts a voice. Six men in uniform appear before you with their weapons drawn. With your own weapons still strapped to your back for the climb, there's nothing you can do. "Hands up," orders the German soldier.

You feel cold and empty as the Germans lead you and your men away. You're a prisoner of war now. You failed in your mission, and life is about to get a lot harder in a German prison camp.

THE END

To follow another path, turn to page 7.
To learn more about the European front, turn to page 100.

The river water is shallow, but it's also ice cold. "Let's find another way," you order. You send Leif and a team of three men in one direction while the rest of the group scouts the opposite way. But after an hour of searching, it's clear that there's no other way across.

"We should move, now," Knut suggests. "We're running out of time."

You slowly nod your head. "Okay, let's move."

The crossing turns out to be easier than you imagined. You're not in the water for a minute before you reach a flat bank on the other side.

Losing so much time is a critical mistake. You still have a lot of ground to cover to reach the target. And before you get there, an orange glow begins to light up the eastern sky. The sun is about to rise.

"We can't attack, not in daylight," Fredrik says.

He's right. You've missed your chance to attack. Instead, you set up a small camp. There, you wait out the day so you can try again at night. But around noon, a German patrol spots you. It's just two men. They run away as soon as they see you.

Turn the page.

As you stare out across the snow-covered forest, you realize that your chance is gone. They'll report you to their superiors. It's likely the Germans will be sending forces out this way within an hour or two. And they'll certainly be stepping up security at the plant.

Your delay cost you the chance to complete your mission. You hang your head as you order the men to pack their gear for the long ski back to safety. You know you'll be returning as a failure.

THE END

To follow another path, turn to page 7.
To learn more about the European front, turn to page 100.

You think about it for a moment. Your orders are to blow up the chambers. But in any operation, you have to be ready to change plans on the fly. The loading station is a much easier target. You can do the damage while putting your men at much lower risk.

"Do it," you say.

Your team moves swiftly, silently swarming over the ground to the nearby loading station. Setting the charges takes just a few minutes. You light the fuses. They're long enough to give you time to get out before the explosions. Hopefully, you'll be long gone before the Germans know what happened.

Turn the page.

"Let's go!" you order. It's a scramble down the cliff. You're back on your skis and headed on a trek toward safe territory long before the explosives go off. Then you hear the blast.

It feels like a victory. But days later, your commanding officer gives you the bad news. "The loading station suffered a lot of damage," he tells you. "But our spies say it will be repaired and working within a week. I'm afraid your mission did almost nothing to slow down the Nazi's atomic research. We can only hope someone else will succeed where you failed."

THE END

To follow another path, turn to page 7.
To learn more about the European front, turn to page 100.

You shake your head. "Our orders were clear. Destroying a loading station won't do enough damage. We have to hit the chambers."

The time is now. You lead the charge. Your team moves swiftly over the snow-covered ground, staying in the shadows to avoid detection.

You're in luck. The Germans have guards posted, but they're watching the bridge. No one thought to guard the plant from the other side.

You arrive at the big chambers and quickly get to work. One by one, you attach charges to the base of each chamber. You set fuses that will delay the explosion and give you time to escape.

Once the last charge is set, it's time to move out. It's back down the cliff and onto your skis as fast as you can move.

Turn the page.

Knut leads the way as you put as much distance as you can between your group and the plant. When the charges finally go off, the blast rattles the ground.

It's a devastating strike. You've completely disabled the heavy water plant. Without the critical fuel, the Nazi atomic program stalls for months.

Your mission is a success! You've played a huge part in keeping the Allies one step ahead of the Axis powers.

THE END

To follow another path, turn to page 7.
To learn more about the European front, turn to page 100.

You don't have lots of time, and you're eager to get started. "Let's move in," you order.

Your team works swiftly to set ropes and begin the dangerous descent down the cliff face. You hoped that you'd be able to move down quickly. But the descent proves challenging.

That slow movement proves costly. When you're about a third of the way down, you hear voices shouting from below. Suddenly, a large searchlight sweeps across the cliff face.

"They've spotted us!" Fredrik shouts.

Within moments, the Germans open fire. You and your men scramble up as fast as you can. Bullets ping off the cliff face. You hear grunts as several of your men are hit—including Leif and Knut.

Turn the page.

You climb frantically. Suddenly, it feels like something bites you in your left thigh. You've been shot.

You can't stop. You press on, ignoring the pain. Finally, you pull yourself over the cliff. In total, five of the 11 team members make it to the top.

"We have to go!" Fredrik shouts. "They'll be sending men up to search for us."

Everyone puts their skis back on and heads out. But your leg slows you down. The men want to wait for you, but it's hopeless. "Go," you order. You can't risk their lives.

You'll do what you can to survive and escape, alone in enemy territory. But even if you survive your wound, can you evade capture by the Germans?

You won't stop fighting. But the odds don't look good. And your mission has been a failure.

THE END

To follow another path, turn to page 7.
To learn more about the European front, turn to page 100.

There's no time to waste. You have to move now. You grab the rope and begin to climb. Within a minute, you hear the sound of approaching voices and the crunch of boots on snow.

"Halt!" shouts a deep voice in German.

You keep climbing. Maybe you can get high enough that you're out of range of their weapons.

"HALT!" shouts the voice again.

The Germans open fire. Leif and a few of the others are higher up the cliff. They're probably safe. But most of your group is still too low. You're sitting ducks here on the cliff face. When the Germans finally open fire, you don't stand a chance. You just hope the explosives you set do enough damage to take down the plant. At least then, the lives of you and your men won't have been wasted.

THE END

To follow another path, turn to page 7.
To learn more about the European front, turn to page 100.

"Everyone, go!" you shout one more time. There's not enough time for all the men to make it up to safety. You've got to give the others a chance.

You charge along the face of the cliff wall. As you run, you draw your weapon and fire rounds into the air to get the attention of the German soldiers.

It works. You hear shouts in German. They're coming at you.

Your legs pump as you work to put as much distance between you and your men as you can. Every step you take brings the German patrol farther from where your men are making their escape.

The sound of gunfire echoes off the cliff face. A bullet pings off the cliff near your head.

You keep running. Every second matters. You won't survive this mission. But the explosives are set, and the Germans won't find them in time to stop them from going off. You can only hope your men make it out alive.

It's not a perfect ending. But you'll take it as a victory.

THE END

To follow another path, turn to page 7.
To learn more about the European front, turn to page 100.

CHAPTER 3

OPERATION TIDAL WAVE

The roar of the B-24 Liberator's engines rattles you in your seat. With your copilot, Ben, by your side, you prepare for takeoff.

You're surrounded by other B-24s. You've been flying these big bomber planes for more than a year. But you've never taken part in a mission quite like this.

"Operation Tidal Wave—I like the name," Ben says as he goes through some preflight checks.

It's an ambitious plan. A huge force of 178 B-24s are set to take off from this airfield in Libya. Your target is more than 1,000 miles away.

It's a huge oil refinery near Ploesti, Romania. The refinery produces much of the fuel for the Axis powers. The plan is simple. Destroy the refinery. Disrupt the flow of fuel to the enemy troops. If you're successful, the mission could cripple the Nazi forces and their supporters.

You and Ben are in the cockpit. Eight more crew members support you in the back. Your navigator, Jack, tracks your location. The rest operate the plane's weapons and other systems.

Dust swirls all around as you take off. The plane, loaded with fuel and bombs, struggles just to get off the ground. You watch as another B-24 tries—and fails—to even take off.

Turn the page.

Ben sighs. "We're barely off the ground and already this mission is a challenge." He's right. It will only get more dangerous from here.

Your radio crackles. It's your squad leader, David. "All right, everyone. It's going to be a long ride. Just remember your orders."

"Maintain radio silence from this moment," he continues. "The element of surprise is critical. Be ready for anything. Good luck."

Slowly, you climb to cruising altitude. It will be hours before you reach your target. But still, your heart is pumping. You know you have a chance to be part of something really big here. You hope you have what it takes.

After the long trip, you begin to approach Romanian airspace. "Let's begin our descent," you tell Ben.

Bringing the plane lower makes you nervous. You've always done your bombing runs from high altitudes. It keeps you safer from most antiaircraft weapons. But your commanders believe the refinery will be heavily defended. They want you to approach it from a very low altitude—just hundreds of feet above the ground.

B-24 Liberators

Turn the page.

"If we stay low, the enemy can't spot us on radar," you tell Ben. "That way, they won't know we're coming until they hear the roar of our engines."

But flying low is dangerous. Jack spots a battery of antiaircraft guns ahead, right along your path. You could veer away from them, but that would separate you from the other planes in your squad. You have to make a quick decision.

- To veer away, go to page 49.
- To hold your course, turn to page 50.

"Banking hard right," you call out as you dip the right wing. The big B-24 is not quick to respond. But you spotted the battery soon enough to steer clear. You watch as the guns open fire, but you're well out of their range.

"This place is really well defended," Ben says. "I have a feeling we're going to be flying right into a lot more of those."

He's right. But there's not much you can do. Your only choices are to press on toward the target, or to break radio silence and warn the other planes that you might be flying into a trap. Neither seems like a very good option.

• To continue on to the refinery, turn to page 55.
• To break radio silence, turn to page 65.

"Holding course," you announce. "It's a risk, but we're coming in low and fast. We won't be an easy target."

You hold your breath as you approach. "Maybe it's not manned," Ben suggests.

For a moment, you think he might be right. Then you spot the flashes as the antiaircraft guns spring into action. The first stream of fire is far off the mark. As the enemy tries to reset, you roar directly over their position. All you need is a few more seconds and you'll be out of their range.

But you're out of luck. The enemy opens fire again. This time, they're on the mark. One of the explosive shells slams into a wing. The plane lurches to the left. You fight to keep it under control.

"Report!" you shout back.

Luis, one of the gunners, announces, "It's bad. Ripped a hole in the left wing. Must have hit a fuel line."

"We're in the heart of enemy territory," Jack says. "If we're going down, get as far south as you can."

You won't be able to keep the plane in the air for long, especially when it's so heavy. There's a long stretch of open, flat plain in front of you. You could dump your cargo and most of your fuel. With a lighter load, you might be able to keep the plane in the air long enough to get to a safer place. Or you could touch down there and take your chances in enemy territory.

- To dump your cargo, turn to page 52.
- To land here, turn to page 59.

You're going down quick, and all the weight you're carrying is only making it faster. "We're too heavy," you call back. "Dump the payload. Dump fuel. Get us lighter!"

Your crew works quickly. As the plane drops weight, your descent slows. Gliding just a few hundred feet above the ground, you veer left. The farther you get from the refinery, the better chance you'll have of evading enemy troops.

Your heart races and you break out in a sweat. The land below you is passing in a flash, even as you slow your speed. Every mile counts.

"There, ahead," Ben calls out.

A straight flat road cuts through the countryside. You head for the road, hoping you have enough time. You're less than 100 feet above the ground now.

Your landing gear touches down just as you align yourself with the road. It's still a rough landing. The unstable plane jerks hard as you touch the ground. But you hold a straight line and bring the big B-24 to a stop. Ben breaks radio silence to call out your position. Maybe somebody can help.

B-24 Liberators flying low over flames

Turn the page.

A grove of trees stands in the distance. "Maybe we should shelter there, out of sight," Jack suggests.

Ben shakes his head. "I think we grab our gear and head west. We get as far away from here as we can, before the Germans arrive." Both men look to you for a decision.

- To take shelter in the trees, turn to page 61.
- To head west, turn to page 63.

"Our orders are clear," you say. "We know the enemy will defend the refinery. That's why we're attacking with so many planes. They can't shoot all of us down."

You continue on your way toward the refinery, flying lower than you've ever flown a B-24 before. It feels strange to see the treetops almost so close that you could reach out and touch them.

Turn the page.

"Target acquired," Jack says. There, before you, lies the refinery. Its big buildings and smokestacks rise up against the horizon. Antiaircraft fire fills the sky. German fighter planes swarm ahead, guns blazing.

You don't slow down a bit. As you scan the scene, you see large storage tanks to your right. The main refinery is dead ahead. But it's well defended, with dozens of antiaircraft guns.

"The refinery is where we can do the most damage," Ben says. "But hitting those tanks would be good too. And a lot safer."

- To drop bombs on the refinery, go to page 57.
- To hit the storage tanks, turn to page 66.

"Hitting those tanks would be easy," you say. "But we want to destroy the refinery itself."

You hold your line, flying into the heart of the enemy defenses.

Suddenly, the plane rattles and shakes.

"We're hit!" Ben cries.

Antiaircraft fire has torn through the tail of your plane. The damage makes the plane difficult to control. But you press forward, fighting to keep yourself in a straight line.

Just as you pass over the refinery, your crew drops its bombs. It's not a perfect hit. Your plane is too unstable to hold the line it needs for a precise strike. But you manage to hit the refinery with a glancing blow. You're sure the explosion has done plenty of damage.

Turn the page.

A B-24 Liberator during Operation Tidal Wave

"We're going down," Ben calls out.

He's right. There's no stopping it. The damage to your plane is too great.

Another section of the refinery stands before you. You have to act fast.

- To crash into the refinery, turn to page 69.
- To try to find a safe place to land, turn to page 71.

Your plane is badly damaged. Even dumping cargo might not get you far, and you may not find a better place to touch down.

"Prepare for emergency landing," you call out. "It might be a rough ride."

The plane dips and lurches as you bring it down. The damaged wing makes it almost impossible to keep it steady. But you do all you can and descend toward the open plain. The ground comes closer and closer. Finally, the landing gear touches down. It's a rough landing. This is no paved airstrip. The plane lurches to the left, tipping as you skid along the ground below.

"Brace yourselves!" you shout. The plane twists and the wing dips until it digs into the ground. Instantly, the plane pivots, driving the nose against the ground.

Turn the page.

Dirt and grass kick up all around you as you plow through the open field. The impact of the crash leaves you dazed. Finally, you realize you've stopped moving—and that you've survived.

Your relief is short-lived. This area is crawling with enemy troops. They will have spotted your crash landing from miles away. By the time you and your crew collect yourselves and get out of the wrecked plane, it's too late. Several dozen enemy soldiers await, each with a weapon drawn.

"Drop your weapons," barks one soldier in a heavy German accent.

You have no choice but to do it. You're a prisoner of war now. You just hope that the mission succeeds without you.

THE END

To follow another path, turn to page 7.
To learn more about the European front, turn to page 100.

Out here in the open, you're completely exposed. "Head for the trees," you tell your men. "Let's get some cover and figure out our best option."

It's a mad dash across the open land. Smoke rises up from the damaged wing of your plane. It's like a beacon to any enemy troops that might be hunting you down.

You feel a little safer once you're in the trees. But your relief is short-lived. The roar of a German fighter plane rattles the ground. You've been spotted.

"We have to get out of here," Jack says. You agree and lead your team in a dash along the edge of the grove. But it's too late. Even as you run, the plane banks and heads back toward you.

Turn the page.

When it arrives, there's nowhere to run. The pilot opens fire, and you know that your contribution to the war effort has come to a tragic end.

THE END

To follow another path, turn to page 7.
To learn more about the European front, turn to page 100.

"We can't stay here," you tell your men. "Everyone grab what you can carry and let's move."

You take a few minutes to gather up what supplies you have—a little food and water, weapons, ammunition, and a radio. Then you strike off west, putting as much distance between you and your crashed plane as you can.

All of you move across the countryside, doing your best to avoid open spaces. Overhead, you spot planes in the air. Some of them are B-24s returning from their bombing mission. Many of them are badly damaged. "I don't think the attack went well," Jack observes.

He's right. The Germans were clearly ready for you. Could they have known the attack was coming?

Turn the page.

Over the next three days, you evade German patrols. Finally, on the third day, Ben makes radio contact with American forces in the area. "Stay put," they tell you. "We'll come get you."

Within an hour, you hear a sound that makes your heart sing. It's the *thump-thump-thump* of an Allied helicopter. The pilot touches down in a nearby field. You and your men rush aboard. Within a few minutes, you're in the air, headed back to safety behind the Allied lines.

Your mission was a failure. Your plane was destroyed. The attack didn't cripple the German fuel lines. But you didn't lose a man. You made it out alive. That's more than a lot of your brothers-in-arms can say.

THE END

To follow another path, turn to page 7.
To learn more about the European front, turn to page 100.

You might be flying into a trap. Your orders are for radio silence, but you just can't do it.

"Alert, alert," you say. "Target is well defended. Low approach not recommended."

It's a mistake. Now the Germans know an attack is coming. Within moments, the sky in front of you lights up with explosions. The enemy is firing with every antiaircraft weapon they have. You have no choice but to break off your course. You can't fly into that.

The good news is that you will survive this mission. The bad news is that you disobeyed orders and put hundreds of other lives at risk. Your military career is over.

THE END

To follow another path, turn to page 7.
To learn more about the European front, turn to page 100.

You veer to your right. "Okay, everyone be ready. I'm heading for that first storage tank. Let's knock it out."

Bullets fly and shells explode all around you as you make your approach. Your low altitude actually gives you some protection. Antiaircraft weapons are designed to hit targets much higher up. It's harder for them to aim at lower targets. You weave through the storm of bullets. "Now!" you shout as you hone in on the storage tank,

Your crew reacts quickly. "Bombs away!" they report.

You pull back on your stick to gain altitude as your bombs hit their target. You can feel the explosions as they hit their marks. "Woo! We got it," Jack says.

Turn the page.

All around you, other B-24s are dropping bombs too. You watch as a few are hit by antiaircraft fire. One just to your left goes down in a ball of flames.

But you have much better luck. You soar over the refinery, climbing and banking left to begin the long voyage back to base.

In the end, the mission is only a partial success. The German defenses stopped the Allied forces from completely destroying the refinery. And many of your fellow airmen never made it back. Still, you know you did your job. You slowed down the Nazi effort—at least a little. And you can't wait until your next chance to hit the enemy where it hurts.

THE END

To follow another path, turn to page 7.
To learn more about the European front, turn to page 100.

You're going down. There's nothing you can do to stop it. It's unlikely you'd survive the crash. And even if you did, you'd be facing death or imprisonment at the hands of the enemy.

You look at your crewmates. Together you decide that there's only one thing to do. You're going down anyway. Maybe you can make your deaths count for something in this awful war.

You press forward on the stick, forcing the plane down even more quickly. It all happens in a flash. Your plane slams into the refinery, sending up a huge ball of flames and doing massive damage. It's a strike that's sure to set the enemy war effort back. Maybe . . . just maybe . . . it will be enough to give the Allies the advantage they need.

Turn the page.

Your adventure has come to an end. You can only hope your sacrifice is worth it.

Damage at the refinery from Operation Tidal Wave

THE END

To follow another path, turn to page 7.
To learn more about the European front, turn to page 100.

Desperately, you pull back on the stick, trying to keep the plane aloft. You scan the ground ahead and aim for a small stretch of open land. The plane shudders and twists as the landing gear touches the ground. The back end spins around, driving a wing into the ground and sending the plane into a barrel roll. It slams into a small building, erupting in a ball of flames.

The mission is only a partial success. Hundreds of airmen, including you, give their lives in the attack. The Nazis quickly repair the damages to the refinery. The supply of oil to the German front lines continues almost uninterrupted. But you died doing all you could to fight back against the advance of the Axis powers.

THE END

To follow another path, turn to page 7.
To learn more about the European front, turn to page 100.

CHAPTER 4

RESCUING THE LOST BATTALION

As you march through the tree-covered slopes of France's Vosges Mountains, you wonder if your mission has any chance of success. The land is rugged, and rain pours down on you. Slogging through the muddy terrain is slow and exhausting. Worse yet, you're moving into the heart of Nazi-occupied territory.

It's October 1944. The war in Europe has stretched on. And now your team, the 442nd Regimental Combat Team, is on what feels like an impossible rescue mission.

Turn the page.

"Move your feet, soldier," barks Captain Stevens. He scowls as he stares you down.

You know he doesn't like you, and you know why. You're a Nisei—a second-generation Japanese American. Your parents came to the United States from Japan. Japan is one of the Axis powers—your enemies in the war.

You were born and raised an American, but your Japanese heritage has made you a target of racism with some of your white commanders and other soldiers.

You're not alone. The 442nd is made up of all Nisei fighters—except for the commanders.

"Don't let him get to you," says Akito, one of your closest friends in the regiment. "Just focus on the mission."

The mission is as important as it is dangerous. The 442nd is one of the units tasked with reaching the 141st Infantry.

The 141st Infantry is called the lost battalion. This group of men has been trapped and is surrounded by enemy forces deep in the mountains. They're running out of food and water. Without help, they're doomed. The Allies' goal is to break through enemy lines and bring the men safely back to Allied territory.

Smoke rises over a nearby peak. It could be Germans.

"You, and you," the captain says, pointing to you and Akito. "Scout ahead. We need eyes on whatever the Germans are up to over that slope."

Turn the page.

"Yes sir!" you reply. The two of you break off from the regiment and head up toward the peak. It's not a steep climb. The mountain is low, and the slope is gentle. You reach the top and scan the valley below you.

Nisei fighters marching

"Oh my," Akito gasps. "There must be a thousand of them down there."

You're not sure it's that many, but there are a lot of men, as well as tanks and artillery. And they're moving in a direction that will intercept your course through the mountains.

The crack of rifle fire echoes through the valley. A shot slams into a nearby tree, sending fragments of wood flying in every direction. A second shot screams right past your ear.

"GET DOWN!" you shout.

Akito cries out in pain. "Ahhh! I'm shot!"

A bullet hit Akito in the lower leg. You grab your friend, supporting his injured leg.

"Come on, we have to get down," you insist.

Turn the page.

The two of you scramble down the mountainside. Akito winces in pain with every step.

A large rock juts out from the side of the mountain. You could hide behind it to give Akito a break. There's a chance the enemy wouldn't spot you there. But if they do, you'd be sitting ducks. Can Akito make it back to your regiment on his injured leg? You're not sure. But you have to act quickly.

- To hide behind the rock, go to page 79.
- To press on down the slope to your regiment, turn to page 80.

"Quick, over there!" you tell Akito. Your friend leans on you as you tuck yourselves behind the rock. You sit quietly for a few moments. In the distance, you hear shouting in German. Slowly, it fades away.

"I think we're safe," you say.

Your friend doesn't look good. He's pale and shivering. He's lost a lot of blood.

You're torn. Your commanders need to know about the German troops as soon as possible. Your regiment could be walking into a surprise attack. Hundreds of lives could be at stake. But Akito needs help now. You could leave him here and send a medic back. But would there be time?

- To stay and help Akito, turn to page 82.
- To go warn your commanders, and send a medic back for Akito, turn to page 84.

"Keep going," you tell Akito. "We can't stop."

Akito is in a lot of pain. You pause for a few moments to tear a strip of fabric from your undershirt and wrap it around his leg.

"This should slow the bleeding," you say.

But every step you take is draining Akito of his energy. About halfway down the slope, he collapses.

"Go on without me," he says through heavy breaths. He looks pale and his eyes have a glassy stare.

He's right. You have to warn everyone. But you can't just leave him here. You have to give him a chance.

You grunt as you grab Akito under the shoulders and haul him to a thick stand of trees. You prop him up against a sturdy trunk, where he's at least safely out of sight.

"Go," Akito says.

• Turn to page 84.

You can't leave Akito. He'll die without help.

"Hold still," you tell him. You use your combat knife to cut one of the sleeves off your shirt. You wrap it tightly just above the bullet wound. "This should stop the bleeding."

You clean the wound as best you can using water from your canteen. After a few minutes, Akito loses consciousness. His vital signs are weak. So you do the only thing you can. You scoop him up and carry him.

It's a long hike back to your unit. By the time your men spot you and Akito, you're exhausted. The medics quickly take over as you collapse to the ground, telling your commander about the German troops.

Your effort is worth it. Under the medics' care, Akito begins to improve. "He'll be all right," one of them tells you. "We'll get him to a field hospital. He should pull through."

• Turn to page 91.

You put your canteen into Akito's hand. "Here, drink this. Keep pressure on your wound. I'll let our commanders know what's ahead and send help back for you."

Akito just nods silently. He closes his eyes and lays down. You take one final look at your friend, hoping it won't be the last time you see him.

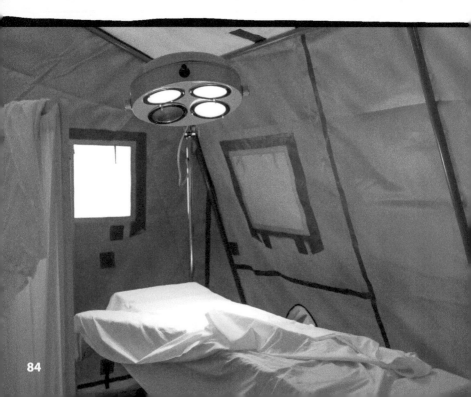

You turn and continue down the slope, weaving through the forest until you reconnect with your regiment.

"Report," says Captain Stevens. You tell him about the German troops, and about Akito. The captain immediately sends medics to the spot you point out.

The march continues through a nearby valley, clear of the German forces. You ask about Akito, but no one has any answers—at least not that they're telling you. You choose to believe that a medical team took him back to a field hospital. But you're afraid that's probably not true.

The time to mourn may come later. For now, you have to stay focused. Your life and the lives of your fellow soldiers depend on it.

Turn the page.

By the next day, you're getting close to the position of the Lost Battalion. After some heavy combat, you break through a weak section of the German lines. It's just what you need to help set the trapped men free.

Scouts have found a German roadblock ahead. A small team of volunteers will attack and destroy it, opening up an escape route. It's a dangerous mission, but it could be the key to victory.

- To volunteer for the attack team, go to page 87.
- To remain with the main force, turn to page 93.

You join a small team of soldiers on the special mission. "The Germans have the road blocked," says one of the officers. "Nobody can get in or out this way. Let's take it down."

You move quietly through the trees, approaching the roadblock in silence. Your fellow soldiers fan out on both sides of you. The roadblock is defended. But the Germans don't know you're coming.

You're part of the explosives team. Your job is to use mortar shells to blow up the roadblock. Other soldiers will rush in during the confusion to deal with the German troops. If you don't successfully accomplish your part of the mission, no one else can do theirs.

Turn the page.

You crouch down, inspecting your target. Your position isn't perfect. A low slope here will make targeting difficult. You could move forward, to flatter ground. But you'd be giving up some of your cover. If the enemy spots you, the entire mission could be doomed.

- To set up here, go to page 89.
- To move forward, turn to page 95.

You can't risk exposing yourself. You'll have to make do with the spot you're in. You carefully set up the mortar and load a shell. You gauge the distance to your target and . . . FIRE!

The enemy never sees it coming. The mortar shot isn't perfect, but it does the job, blasting right through the roadblock. In an instant, the rest of your team attacks, taking advantage of the enemy's surprise and confusion. The battle lasts only a few minutes. It's a success! The roadblock is destroyed. As quickly as you came, you disappear back into the trees. You return to your unit and report that the road is clear.

Captain Stevens gives you a rare smile and slaps you on the back. "Good work, soldier," he says.

• Turn to page 91.

Soldiers loading field artillery

The real battle begins the next day. The German forces in the area are ready and well positioned for a fight. According to rumors, Nazi leader Adolf Hitler himself ordered that the Lost Battalion not be rescued at all costs. You'll have to fight for every inch of ground. Your orders are to break through the German lines and open up an escape route.

Shots echo over the wooded landscape as the fighting begins. Your regiment, along with several others, work side by side. The fighting is intense. Explosions rock the ground all around you. But you keep pushing forward.

In the chaos of battle, you lose track of your unit. You don't recognize anyone around you.

Turn the page.

There are American soldiers with you, but they're not from your unit. Should you keep fighting alongside these men? Or should you fall back and try to find your own unit?

- To keep fighting, turn to page 96.
- To fall back, turn to page 98.

"This is it, men" explains Captain Stevens. "We've split into two main groups. We're going to attack together to break the enemy lines."

Your heart is racing. You've seen combat in the months since you joined the war effort. But this will be a true close-in battle. It will be dirty, bloody, and more dangerous than anything you've ever done.

A slow rain falls as you begin your advance up the hill. You stand next to Toshiro Urabe, one of your unit's best fighters. Your stomach is in knots. But Urabe is ready—like a boxer going into the ring.

With a loud, "WHOOP," Urabe leads the charge. You grasp your weapon with its long, sharp bayonet at the end and join in.

Turn the page.

Soon the entire unit is screaming and running up the hill, right into the enemy defenses. It's complete madness. You aren't sure if you're being incredibly brave or just crazy. But you get swept up in the moment. With your fellow soldiers at your side, you feel almost invincible.

You crash into the enemy lines. All around you, fighting rages. German and American soldiers fall by the dozens. You last longer than most. But this isn't the sort of battle many people survive. Your mad charge plays a big role in breaking the German lines and rescuing the Lost Battalion. Sadly, you aren't there to celebrate the victory.

THE END

To follow another path, turn to page 7.
To learn more about the European front, turn to page 100.

You want to have a good shot. You inch forward on your hands and knees, through the mud and brush, to find the best possible spot.

You're so close now that you can hear the German troops talking. You work quickly, setting up the mortar and preparing to fire. But everything is wet from constant rain. You fumble as you load the shell into the mortar. Metal clangs loudly against metal. In an instant, the Germans are on high alert. Rifle fire rings out.

You try again, desperately trying to load the shell. But you've been spotted. Your cover is blown, and the Germans open fire. If the Lost Battalion is going to be saved, it will be without you.

THE END

To follow another path, turn to page 7.
To learn more about the European front, turn to page 100.

You don't know which regiment these men are from, but it doesn't matter. As the battle rages around you, sticking with fellow Allied soldiers is all that matters.

The group of soldiers is surging forward to secure a hill. You join in, rushing ahead to clear the way. Behind you, Allied forces are launching artillery shells. The explosions send dirt flying into the air.

Just as you're about to reach the hilltop, a shell explodes near you. The sound of the blast is deafening. A sharp pain shoots through your whole body.

You fall to the ground. It takes a moment for you to realize that you've been hit by a piece of shrapnel from the blast. A sharp, hot piece of metal has buried itself in your lower back. The pain is intense.

You can only lie there as the battle plays out. You drift in and out of consciousness. Finally, after the Allies have broken through the German lines, medics arrive. They immediately start tending to your wound.

All around you, soldiers are hooting and hollering. "What happened?" you ask.

The medic smiles. "We broke through, soldier. We freed the Lost Battalion. You've got a long recovery ahead of you, but you can be proud of your contribution. Well done!"

THE END

To follow another path, turn to page 7.
To learn more about the European front, turn to page 100.

Even as the men around you surge forward, you drop back. You scan the battlefield for your men. Smoke hangs over the scene in front of you as explosions blow craters into the ground.

Finally, you spot familiar faces. Reunited with your unit, you continue the fighting.

It's chaos as the Allies push the German line to the breaking point. A round of artillery shells opens up a huge gap in the line. The charge is on. You join hundreds of U.S. soldiers as you rush forward, splitting the German defenses in two.

It's the turning point. For the first time, the Lost Battalion isn't surrounded. As other regiments continue the fight, yours pushes forward. You scale a tree-covered ridge until you finally reach the 211 U.S. soldiers who have been trapped there for so long.

They're exhausted, hungry, and close to collapse. But seeing you brings smiles to their faces and tears to their eyes. You've done it. The fight has cost countless lives. And it will go on long after these men are safe. But today has been a huge victory.

THE END

To follow another path, turn to page 7.
To learn more about the European front, turn to page 100.

CHAPTER 5
A BLOODY CAMPAIGN

World War II was one of the bloodiest wars in human history. An estimated 15 million soldiers died in combat, and another 25 million were wounded. Even worse, the war took the lives of 45 million civilians. Some of the most intense fighting was along the European—or Western—front. Early in the war, Germany and its allies acted quickly, taking over key territories and rapidly expanding its power.

The Allies, including the United Kingdom, France, the United States, and the Soviet Union, fought back. As the years passed, the Allies slowly pushed the Germans back. The war was waged on the ground, in the air, and at sea.

Huge battles, such as the invasion of Normandy, the Battle of the Bulge, and the Battle of Berlin served as turning points in the war. But those battles tell only part of the story.

It was a constant struggle between the Allies and Axis powers to fuel and supply troops and keep up the best possible intelligence. Rescue missions, spy operations, and supply chain disruptions all played important roles in the war.

After six years of fighting, the Allies finally closed in on victory. By April 1945, the German capital of Berlin was surrounded.

Adolf Hitler

American and British forces closed in from the West, while Soviet forces came in from the East. Germany had lost. They had no choice but to surrender. Nazi leader Adolf Hitler took his own life rather than be captured.

The war in Europe was over. However, the battle in the Pacific carried on. Japan refused to surrender to the Allies.

As the death toll mounted, the United States took a drastic step. It unleashed a new weapon of terrible power. U.S. bombers dropped the first atomic bomb on the Japanese city of Hiroshima on August 6, 1945. They dropped a second one on Nagasaki three days later. Both cities were destroyed. Hundreds of thousands of people died.

Japan was defeated. It soon surrendered, and World War II was over. Yet the effects of the war echoed throughout the decades. Germany was split in half. New lines were drawn. The United States and the Soviet Union had fought as allies during the war. But after it, they became enemies. Each built up its own arsenal of atomic weapons, leaving the world on the brink of destruction.

Almost 80 years later, the divide between the East and the West remains. The Soviet Union dissolved in 1991. Russia—the largest part of the Soviet Union—continued to distrust the West. In 2022, Russia started a bloody war against Ukraine. Their goal was to stop the United States and its allies from expanding into former Soviet territory. The devastating war is just another sign that the effects of World War II carry into the modern day.

MAP OF EUROPEAN FRONT 1939

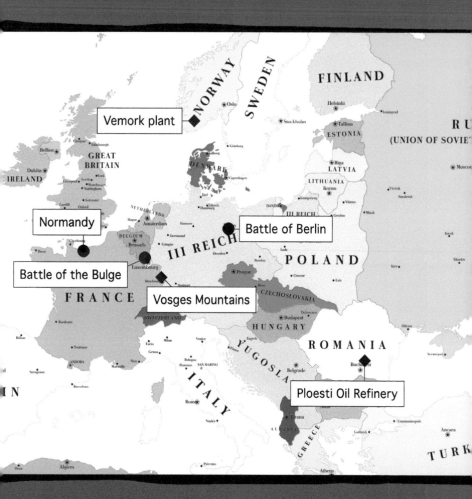

Vemork plant

Normandy

Battle of Berlin

Battle of the Bulge

Vosges Mountains

Ploesti Oil Refinery

LEGEND

● BATTLES

◆ POINTS OF INTEREST

TIMELINE

+ **Sept. 1, 1939**   Germany invades Poland. World War II begins.

+ **Dec. 7, 1941**   Japanese planes bomb Pearl Harbor, Hawaii. The next day, the United States enters the war.

+ **Feb. 27, 1943**   Norwegian forces attack a German-controlled heavy water plant, badly damaging it.

+ **Aug. 1, 1943**   Allied forces launch Operation Tidal Wave.

+ **Oct. 1944**   U.S. forces drive into German-held territory in France's Vosges Mountains to rescue the Lost Battalion.

+ **Dec. 16, 1944**   German forces launch a surprise attack on the Allied line, called the Battle of the Bulge.

+ **Jan. 1945**   The Allies drive back the Germans, putting down the Nazi's last major offensive of the war.

+ **May 7, 1945**   Germany surrenders, ending the war in Europe.

+ **Aug. 1945**   U.S. bomber planes drop atomic bombs on the Japanese cities of Hiroshima and Nagasaki. Japan surrenders a few days later.

OTHER PATHS TO EXPLORE

In this book, you've explored several key operations that took place on the European front during World War II. But the experiences of those who fought in these situations where just a part of what it was like to live and serve, during World War II. How might your perspective change in a different situation?

1. Women weren't allowed to serve in combat roles during World War II. But that doesn't mean they didn't contribute to the war effort. What sort of jobs might women have taken to help in the war? How could they have helped without actually fighting directly?

2. Nisei fighters were second-generation Japanese soldiers. But Japan was a member of the Axis powers. Imagine being a white soldier fighting alongside the Nisei. Would you trust them? Or would you understand that their Japanese heritage makes them no less American?

3. The Allies relied on spies to provide critical war information. Spies often worked in, or alongside, enemy armies. What would it feel like to secretly live among enemy forces. Would it be hard to remain loyal if you interacted every day with your enemies? Can you imagine what it would be like living in constant fear of being discovered?

GLOSSARY

altitude (AL-ti-tood)—the height of something above sea level or Earth's surface

artillery (ar-TIL-uh-ree)—large guns, such as cannons or missile launchers, which require several soldiers to work them

atomic (uh-TOM-ic)—using the power created when atoms are split

battalion (buh-TAL-yuhn)—a unit of personnel in the armed forces

heritage (HARE-uh-tij)—the culture and traditions of one's family, ancestors, or country

mortar (MOR-tur)—a short cannon that fires shells or rockets high in the air

navigator (NAV-uh-gay-tuhr)—someone who plans an airplane's flight path; navigators read maps for pilots

Nazi (NOT-see)—a member of the political party of Germany, led by Adolf Hitler, which ruled Germany from 1933 to 1945

payload (PAY-lohd)—the total weight of items carried by an airplane; in war, missiles and bombs

refinery (ri-FINE-uh-ree)—a place where oil is turned to fuel

regiment (REHJ-uh-mehnt)—a military unit made up of many sections

SELECT BIBLIOGRAPHY

Badsey, Stephen (ed.). *The Hutchinson Atlas of World War II Battle Plans: Before and After.* Chicago: Helicon Publishing, 2000.

Bascomb, Neal. *The Winter Fortress: The Epic Mission to Sabotage Hitler's Atomic Bomb.* New York: Houghton Mifflin, 2016.

Go For Broke National Education Center goforbroke.org/rhineland-campaign-rescue-of-the-lost-battalion/

Schneider, Carl J. and Dorothy Schneider. *World War II.* New York: Facts on File, 2003.

Suermondt, Jan. *Infantry Weapons of World War II.* Minneapolis: Chartwell Books, 2012.

WW II in HD watch.historyvault.com/shows/wwii-in-hd?cmpid=HV_WWIIHD_Site_Promo_Tile

Zaloga, Steven J. *Ploesti 1943: The Great Raid on Hitler's Romanian Oil Refineries.* London: Bloomsbury, 2019.

READ MORE

Dickmann, Nancy. *Fighting to Survive World War II: Terrifying True Stories.* North Mankato, MN: Compass Point Books, 2020.

Doeden, Matt. *What If You Were on the Russian Front in World War II?: An Interactive History Adventure.* North Mankato, MN: Capstone Press, 2023.

MacCarald, Clara. *Weapons of World War II.* Lake Elmo, MN: Focus Readers, 2023.

INTERNET SITES

Ducksters: World War II
ducksters.com/history/world_war_ii/

History for Kids: World War II
historyforkids.net/world-war-two.html

The National World War II Museum
nationalww2museum.org/learn/education/for-students/

ABOUT THE AUTHOR

Matt Doeden is a freelance author and editor from Minnesota. He's written numerous children's books on sports, music, current events, the military, extreme survival, and much more. His books *Basketball Shoes, Shorts, and Style*; *Dragons*; and *Could You Be a Monster Wave Surfer?* (all by Capstone Press) are Junior Library Guild selections. Doeden began his career as a sportswriter before turning to publishing. He lives in Minnesota with his wife and two children.